T0164214

Through the Hourglass

Through the Hourglass

POEMS OF
LIFE AND LOVE

JOHN A. CALHOUN

ILLUSTRATIONS BY SUE LYN ANDERSON GIOULIS

Bartleby Press
Washington • Baltimore

Printed in the United States of America

Published and distributed by:

Bartleby Press

8600 Foundry Street
Mill Box 2043
Savage, Maryland 20763
800-953-9929
www.BartlebythePublisher.com

ISBN 978-0-910155-85-4
Library of Congress Control Number: 2010942123

To the nurturers of the next generation

Contents

Preface

The fact that a national magazine, *Town & Country*, published my poem "Ledge" does not make me a poet. The fact that many of my friends tell me that they enjoy and look forward to my poems, sometimes even passing them along, does not make me a poet. So what does?

Perhaps it is simply that this particular form suits me best as I struggle to get to the heart of the matter, a sudden glimpse of the extraordinary under the ordinary, my constant wonder at and commitment to family and friends. Poetry should not be coy, trying to hide meaning in odd lines and strange rhythms. For me it is the opposite: I want the reader to come with me into the heart of the emotion, to the wonder and emotion I feel.

Through this form I try, as husband, parent and now grandparent, to convey amazement, discovery, delight, and a sense of celebration (for it is transitory). By embracing a single situation, a poem also fits me as I give tribute to the larger family to which we all belong. We cannot and do not exist alone. We are connected to, sustained through, and inspired by the examples of friends and others who touch our lives, sometimes unwittingly, like toothless Rose, who begs on 17th and K Streets in Washington, D.C., who drinks Diet Coke "to keep my figure," and who despite outward signs of collapse, gives us a precious glimpse of her core spark.

The arc of this book begins with Courting and my earliest poems, love poems for the newly met, not-yet-my-wife Ottilia. She, a teacher and resident of a small apartment in Fort Lee, New Jersey, lived within sight and sound of the George Washington Bridge. As we dated, the trips out from Manhattan along piers sticking out into the Hudson River evoked piano keys for me, and the rhythmic thump of the taxi wheels provided percussion for "Westside Drive: 2:00 AM" The poems of our courtship are accompanied by three of the same period, poems inspired by our budding relationship.

Then poems on married life and our young children, Byron and Hollis, usher in the Golden Age of Parenting. This is the era of "Dad, watch me!" and of adventures together, stories at night, the desire to snuggle close, the seeing all as glitteringly new. "Hand-holds" and "Tides" exult in their growing confidence, competence and caring, dimly foreshadowed by the sense that they will all too soon be off on their own.

I begin their teen years by poetry celebrating their limitless energy and the boundary pushing that crashes against our settled, adult shores in "Teen Challenge." My exultation cedes soberly to the reality that teens need to push away in order to discover themselves. At this stage they don't know who they are, and so define themselves by who they are not. "Kite" reflects that painful day at the summer beach house that could not contain us all: the kite string snapping. "Spring?" describes the trying times for a marriage when work, shuttling to sports and plays, school and the struggle to get homework done, and the struggle to pay bills can make a marriage more a business than a union, a focused partnership in which one can forget, as we did for a time, the core passion that began it all.

In another poem in this section, I reach out to connect with my son, whose love of literature took him to James Joyce and led me to write "Upon Giving Ellmann's James Joyce to My Son." Thankfully, we persisted through these sometimes turbulent years.

I wrote "Silver Anniversary Sonnet" and "Grace" as quiet benedictions to the return of the essence of what we were and are as a family. And a bit of pure fun: birthday and other holiday poems are a staple of our family tradition, and so I include "Valentine Sonnet for Hollis."

Next, the Miracle of Grandchildren. The gift of grandkids brings me back to the earliest days with my children in full flood: new life, new worlds, new joys of discovery. I'm on the floor again, again playing Fish, building sand castles, wrestling, telling stories, getting homemade pizza sauce all over the kitchen, and again, my God again, *Curious George.* My grandchildren, Lauren and Katie, serve as muses for such poems as "Sidewalk Cracks," "Wondering Along," and "Summer at the Beach."

In Portraits, I describe friends whose lives interweave with ours or others who simply (but profoundly) offer inspiration and connection. They reflect the amazing spark of the divine in each of us, and the hope, often undeclared, pushing and elevating us. "Rose" is conjoined with the fate of a pre-teen son of a friend who barely survives a car crash but struggles back to normalcy. The guitarist in "Musician on Boston's Blue Line" apologizes to a dead composer and a clutch of awestruck passengers for his one missed note in a tangled fugue as he strives to reach Bach's ideal, and reminds us all to "play on...and on...." "George" swims hard through, but not above, his childhood of abuse, inspiring us all. In "Dirt" I celebrate the competent, courageous and unfailingly committed colleagues and friends who do the brutally difficult work of trying to prevent youth violence, thereby allowing those on the edge to reach their potential and to improve the communities in which they live. I try to convey the sudden and surprise spark of the transcendent in "A Sparrow at Dulles Airport."

The last section, Going and Coming, opens with thoughts on the illness and death of close friends linked with the new life at the other end of life. Here I contrast Mike's last days with the baptism of my granddaughter Katie. "Zyg" examines the 10-by-15-foot room that is now the universe of this esteemed world citizen. Has all tragically shrunk to this tiny nook, or has it expanded because of the constant love expressed by a train of family and friends who stream in to visit him? Small physical space or limitless, unquestioning love, beyond word, beyond and deeper than any worldly accomplishment?

My book concludes with "Mother" and "Imago Dei," two poems that raise the same question: "Why do we wait so long—often until a person is dying—to express love for another? What's the risk? Why the timidity?" We are all loved by and made in the image of God, and thus should be emboldened to love despite fear of rejection or loss. In love we are confirmed and by love we are commissioned.

Although contained by the hourglass, I believe that life is shaped by and always pulls us toward love and connection. Because of love and connection we transcend the confines of the hourglass: That message is the heart of my book.

John A. Calhoun
Falls Church, Virginia
December 2010

Courting

Westside Highway 2:00 AM

Dock-pier
Dock-pier
     Xylophone keys into the Hudson.
Dock-pier
Dock-pier
     Hard rubber drumming cobbled cement.

Then glissando up the ramp
to the bridge
where they'd turned on the lights for us,
stringing them down and then
up
and up and up where
fog covered and halo'd the top ones.
The bridge a tuning fork in soft hum.

Dock-pier-bridge
Dock-pier-bridge
Sweepfog.
Play it!
Oh yes,
Play it!

New York City, September 1970

3

Urban Robin

A crazy robin woke me up at
6:30 this morning in 8-track stereo.
Its lone voice dimensioned
off all those cement walls.

Someone upstairs threw
an old slipper at the bird,
which flew up a few branches
without breaking chirping stride.

After a while I got to like that bird.
I didn't know whether his breast was full
of pain or joy or what,
but I do know that I heard him above the traffic
crowding onto the George Washington Bridge,
and I do know that he refused to be intimidated
by all that cement.

New York City, September 1970

Because of Isness

Now there is an
isness
that we've got to find out about,
for
I'm not Eastern enough to say
isness is
everness is
alwaysness,
just waiting in the celestial wings for yesness.

My Westernness
pushes me to motion and choice,
because if we don't plunge into the heart of
potential isness,
it just might become
wasness,
or might-have-been niceness
(floating away on Eastern mists of who-knowsness).

This is to say, then,
that it takes a bit of
Westernness to find out about
isness,
meaning that I'm very glad that we're to be living together
to find out about
isness and whether
isness
could be carried, live and loving,
ahead daily to a
maybe
usness.

New York City, November 1970

Wild Flower

The seed
> blown a tortuous route landed on
> new ground and grabbed hard for a root
> in

The earth,
> which it surprised
> but which slowly shifted to make room and to nourish
> as

The water
> cooperated, loosening the grudging soil
> softening the resistant shell, while
> birthing

The stem
> probing, light green,
> to break through to the warming light and
> into

The wind,
> which tested it, tugged,
> and threw all sorts of weather
> at it.

Some
> saw it, knelt, and cupped its youth
> in wondering hands reflecting the awe
> of promise.

Others
> would come unseeing with heavy boots
> or cutting shears or perhaps
> bulldozers.

Most

        would not see or would not care
        that the answer lay
        in

The soil

        in which there was a root fingering deep
        into the dark and thrusting up a dancing stem that
        was already daring a bud.

New York City, October 1970

Cosmic Bed

I watch you sleep
and see only your blond head and
a tip of your elbow,
extending from a large wrinkle,
which is you,
in a 4 by 6 bed.

A wrinkle.
How little space we take up in this world!
But how the world crowds in with us!
Filled with it we leap for joy
or possessed by it,
we're brought to our knees.

Move over, world.
Let us be, for just a little while,
a wrinkle.
Move over.
Let us be.
Just us.

Cambridge, Massachusetts, November 1970

Kids

Fast Ride
Balance
Tides
Handholds
White Pine
Of Windmills and No Socks

Fast Ride

Red cheeks flecked by Kleenex snow.
Streaking scarves underline shouts of glee.

Balls of ice dangle from curly hair,
wondrous cotton structures frieze excited faces.

We mount up – doubles, triples, quadruples,
with Hollis rolling off first, intrepid she,
looking like she'd plowed into whipped cream.

Cousin Doug hit the fence twice and bounced back
like a football player tackled head on, dazed.

The hill beckoned sleds with irresistible lure,
greater than French fries and a hamburg with ketchup.

They didn't pee for three hours.

That astounding moment – Byron's streak of color,
a smile sailing down a snowy hill – infinitely more –
a glimpse through the curtain of eternity.
Too much to bear.

The transcendent moment overwhelms.
Maybe God helps us and has them grow,
pushing against us.
So we won't die of the pain.

McLean, Virginia, January 1983

11

Balance

Your flesh is depleted.
There is more of pajama material and less of you.

I carry you downstairs to see the squirrel –
a break from the hot, flowered pillow,
the rumpled bed,
the flat Coke,
the barf bowl resting on the faded towel,
and the silent sentinels: Sudafed, Triaminic, and Robitussin.

Your cheek hot against mine, you giggle at the adventure –
this brazen trip of ten yards –
to look at a squirrel through the kitchen window.
Your constant well of joy, even in sickness,
pushing up a sticky smile, revealing
six-year-old teeth, unbrushed, uneven.

The squirrel's flesh is full,
his snug coat in consonance with his body,
his tail a snapping lash of tension and alertness,
undeterred by last night's storm.
He has nosed a wake in the snowy sea,
uncovering the seeds we'd scattered
and lurching up, paws clasped,
he
nibbles serenely,
darting eyes the sole
betrayer of
his prayerful pose.

"Why isn't he cold?" Hollis asks.
"Out in the snow. All alone."

"Look, he's fat," I say. "Look at his fur coat.
That keeps him warm."

"But how can he be in the cold snow and warm
and I'm hot but cold?"

"Your body's out of balance," I explain.
"There's a battle in your body, good germs against bad.
It's a hot fight
That makes you warm.
But that fight makes you weak, too,
so you shake and get chilly.
The squirrel's body is in balance.
He's not sick.
His heart and blood make him warm.
His fur coat keeps the warmth in –
like a fireplace in a snug house."

She's breathing fast, fighting for balance, head on my shoulder,
eyeing the riddle of the warm animal in the snow.
"I'm cold, Daddy.
Hold me tight. I need you for a coat."

McLean, Virginia, February 1984

13

Tides

You cling to me like a barnacle
as we fight to get out.
We are joined. One.
We shoulder through the medium waves,
duck under the big, and drift with the small.
We are now beyond the breakers.
The lifeguard stands anxiously in his chair.
He has whistled once.

Now we ride!
Forces unseen lift us off the sea floor.
We float over the top.
We have to know the rhythm and the forces and
we must trust them.
Down we slide.
Picked up again, we bob as gulls on the incessant swells.
"Ride over the top. Don't fight it. Don't worry.
The wave will bring you right back to me."

I push you off.
You are on your own.
The burgeoning water hill embraces you, easing you high.
Into God's Hand?
A tiny wheat seed in His Back 40?
I look hard to distinguish your blond head
among the tatters of light in the dark waters
you, framed in the rising swell,
a precious animal trapped for an eternal moment in amber.
Your triumphant grin hardens to worry as you are
pulled into a sucking trough.
Don't fight. Just keep your head up.
The next wave is coming. It will work for you.
The wave will carry you into my arms.
Trust me.

Trust me.
You trust me. I trust me and my knowledge
as these unseen rhythms
pick us up off our feet,
as wind the leaves.
Your anxious look softens as the trough levels.
The wave then grows,
stopping your back drag,
lifting you, carrying you
into my arms.
You chortle with relief and delight;
your cheek is plastered to mine.
This time you look out to the sea, away from land,
To do it again.

Each time I take your feet,
launching you into the mounting wall,
but today, the third day, you push my arms aside.
You swim into the awesome water wall alone.

Now you smile in the trough.
You know you will be brought into my arms.
And you are.
Now you trust yourself.

Soon, all too soon,
you will neither start in my arms
nor return to them.
You will confront walls alone.

But will you launch someone from your arms?
Will you teach trust?
I am giving you knowledge
and trust.

Hopefully joy.
But have I given you caring as well?

Swim, my daughter,
oh swim!

Avalon, New Jersey, August 1981

Handholds

You are so much quicker at scaling than I had thought.
There is much circumspection in you.
I showed you how to find handholds,
to test them gently,
not all weight at once;
to make sure,
and then to find a foothold
and move up and up.

The ocean rolls beneath us and
pulling back reveals
rocks and seaweed.
There is certainty in the Maine rock,
not the dry crumble of the Southwest.

We look for stairs and chimneys,
but you prefer the straight face climbs.

You shout gleefully when you find the rare loose rock.
You, so proud of discovery
and growing sense of consequence,
throw the offending rock into the sea.

The next day your sister comes.
You teach:
"You have to find a handhold and a foothold.
Both!"
Then "Let's try to find a loose rock.
That's how you can get hurt."

I hoist you up and
you feel a neat path as

the sea below us roars.
Amazing how you see only your thread ladder in front of you
as the cosmos shakes and
we get damp from spray.

You ascend another ledge.
You first, then Hollis,
then I, the catcher.
"Daddy, I've found good places.
You don't have to catch."
"Just in case," I say.
"Anything can happen.
I'm your net.
Keep going."
Launch and catch.
Catch.
Then launch again.

How I want you to climb!
But how I never want to stop
catching.
Suddenly your sneaker disappears
over the ledge above me.
I feel the pit of my stomach.
Do I really want to launch you
beyond my reach?

No.
I quickly find the cracks, the handholds,
places for feet,
going up and up to the air where the sneaker was.
I, catcher, now pursuer.

Suddenly your face consumes the ice-blue sky.
You lean over.
"There are two good handholds.
One over here.
Another near my chin."

You point to a tiny ledge above my right hand.
I look up at my young son
and I do not hear
the sea.
Catcher, launcher, each.
We are coming full circle.

Georgetown, Maine, September 1981

White Pine

That night the storm ripped the top
off the huge hickory, it landed on
our Christmas pine, the only white pine.
If it wasn't a twister, then what do you call
a wind that tears out front door,
topples trees, and moves parked cars?

In the eerie calm and drizzle,
I went out about 11:00 p.m.,
my flashlight finding the other two firs
ringed by fallen branches but erect, unharmed.
Heaped where the white pine should have been
(and we knew because we'd planted it together)
a pile of steaming, broken hickory.

I shouted for Byron, for he'd chosen that pine.
We'd dug together, planted deeply, and
watered during the dry winter (last year's tree had died).
This one had thrived. I held out hope:
"Pines bend. If the trunk's not split, we can save it."

We sawed a rough hickory circle around the unseen pine,
wet leaves slapping our faces,
slick branches blackening our arms.
Now sensing the center we worked furiously.
Branches snapped.
A gentle rain fell steadily.
I remember raindrops dripping from his hair.

We cleared a hole, yanking debris aside,
fully exposing the pine to the glare of our flashlight –
a patient.
Byron leaped to the horribly angled tree,
felt up and down the wrinkled bark and shouted
"It's not split. We saved it!"

We slapped a wet five,
then slowly straightened and
tightly roped the pine to a six-foot steel stake
torn from my garden.

We stood quietly in the rain
looking at our white pine,
feeling roots.

McLean, Virginia, October 1986

Of Windmills and No Socks

The dull snow sky is
flecked by falling leaves,
kicked by the wind and
chased by my daughter
who bursts inside
to check out her brother.

"Our thing was white socks," I recall.
"White socks! That's OK with sneakers,
but not with loafers. They'd think you're a nerd."
No socks.
"And shirttail out?"
"Yeah. Most of the guys wear it out.
Nerdie is tucked in."

"Let me check you, Byron," Hollis appraises.
"Are you going to dance?
Are your friends going to dance?
You look nice, but wait…turn around."
She pats down an errant wisp of hair.
He hammerlocks, then actually hugs her.
We watch him go.

We raid the fridge, dance to Scott Joplin,
Hollis with my Burpee hat low on her face.
I conduct from behind her, flapping her arms.
She folds to the floor in laughter.

That afternoon, huddled over her *Animal Farm* project,
She says "I can't draw a windmill."
Mom digs out a book that gives her a good picture.
The wind roars.
Leaves scrape against the windows.
My daughter draws windmills and

my son, with starched shirt
pressed pants, and
slicked hair is somewhere
at his first boy/girl party.

That night, we race to visit Aunt Peggy in the hospital.
Four days after hip surgery and resulting plate,
Peggy is too tired to say much except "good night."
Almost asleep, crowded by walker and toilet,
she hardly hears my kids careening down the hall
in her wheelchair.

We leave, run down the steep hill
to the parking lot, tackling, rolling,
even somersaulting.

We sing on the way home.
I watch them race around the yard under a full moon,
trying to catch spinning leaves torn from trees.
My children
exploding into teen years.

McLean, Virginia, October 1988

Teens

Teen Challenge

Things break.
Incessant phone calls shatter dinner.
Cereal litters kitchen counters.
Clothes cover floors.
To be a teen is to strew.

They run, careen, but never seem to walk.
They bump into others, sometimes with meaning.

Their energy slams at the boundaries of
bodies,
rooms,
parents,
teachers.

They disdain compromise.
Doors slam.
Walls shake.
Voices rise.
They are compelled to batter the world.

Would we really want it otherwise,
these birth pangs of this
next generation?

Is this not the rarest of times?
Pre-calculation.
Pre-marriage.
Pre-compromise.
When challenge is fully dared;
When the dream tide swells,
unbound by decades
of expectation and habit.

Their inexorable push
washes on our settled shores,
sometimes exulting in the sound
of itself crashing;
sometimes bringing cleansing waters,
nutrients to depleted shores.

We can either
construct desperate sea walls,
or
let in the tide.

Fifty years can give wisdom.
Fifty years can ossify.
Let those waves crash!
Unsettle the compacted sand
of my known world.

McLean, Virginia, November 1990

Upon Giving Ellmann's James Joyce to My Son Byron

RevelByrevel!
Jump for Joy ce!
Beat waxing wings
'Gainst McLeanMcLangleyMcBurbiaMcByre of
Birth bedding

SoarSonsoar!
Sidelysweepsshatteredshards of
Pinions past.

WarySonwary!
Witting, wiley weave waxed wings with
Your wicked wonderous will;
and
Warpwoofs of love.

ByeBybye!
But ever, Icarus-like
Land lauding
Peoplesong to again
Later leap.

Andover, Massachusetts, February 1993

Kite

Exultant words joying
from the five-year-old,
red sunset spangling
his blond hair:
"Dad, dad it's up!"
These words oh these words snatch me back to
"Dad, let's play catch…"
"Dad, watch me ride the waves…"
"Dad, wrestle with me…"
"Dad, let's race…"--
from me the past and
blood from my heart.

Exultant red diamond yanking
a lightly leashed puppy,
lurching, tailsnapping, snaking, veering, skewing, straining
against string and ocean breeze.

Exultant you kite-launched into life's winds,
you pullingexploringtuggingalwaystuggingleaning
headlong into uncharted skies.
Parental string slacking,
then you spinning, diving.
We tightening the string, righting you
again to soar.

Exultant flyer – math, music, baseball, books, friends;
careening into doubt and know,
but then suddenly on that August day
Youwindyouscreamingwavespounding,
grabbed, ripped, tore away string,
and now
disappear over the horizon, a smalling
red dot (your father's blood)
and with it a whispered blessing
muffled by roar.

Bethany Beach, Delaware, August 1993

Valentine Sonnet for Hollis

Long-legged, laughing daughter of mine,
careening to birthday sixteen;
on winter's day you're a Valentine,
the best there's ever been.

Loyal and steadfast to those near you,
(you'll never let one down).
Your room bursts with music, laughs of your crew
as you gather all around.

Under joyous jangle of all that's new
live verities not in contest.
To all friends stays the essential you:
Ally, wit and unslacking zest.

So hail, daughter, with spirit so plucky!
The awaiting world is very lucky!

McLean, Virginia, February 1993

Spring?

We created spring and flung seeds wild
and naught was wrong and no thing defiled.

Grace sparked every step and small was small.
We feared nothing – laughed, embracing all.

Of spring's "yes" and profligacy
came summer's crop, offspring of you and me.

Fall was hard. The reaping, work, a test.
We sweated; by toil was love compressed.

Friends said the crop was wondrous rich,
but we didn't know how much we had missed.

Our yield partly in, a light snow fell;
spring slipped away from our sylvan dell.

Snuck away! We didn't see it go!
for our eyes were down on earth and hoe.

We forgot to pause in gratitude
and link soiled hands in true beatitude.

The ground then iced; the snow came deep.
We looked only to house and to our keep.

We forgot about seeds and leaping spring;
neglected our love, our song to sing.

Now ask as winter's hand of dread
Yields to thaw: Are seeds dormant now or dead?

The stubble stands—as promise? as pall?
Let us seek the seed that launched it all.

McLean, Virginia, Valentine's Day 1993

Silver Anniversary Sonnet

Know that silver is solid, heavy, true,
but despite its heft can yield to tarnish,
and that its gleam by encroaching black would sue.
So with stout heart we would ebon varnish.

Quarter century – about twice twelve –
we've traveled life's path of children, jobs, home,
and amid the surface commotion now delve
beneath the silver – to the marrow, to the bone.

For then your luster caught my roving eye, and yours mine –
and before God, friends, and family,
together we vowed bejeweled sympathy –
to link arms, souls, life, for eternity.

It's what's under soot and the work we make,
to scour grime, the precious silver to retake.

McLean, Virginia, May 1996

35

Grace

We played a lot of tennis that summer.
Every morning my
heels ached,
knees creaked,
back locked,
serving arm sagged limp as pasta.
My son's shots exploded;
he caught balls on the fly,
covered the court like a gazelle,
jumped over the net between games,
and scaled fences to retrieve errant balls.

Before he left for school I wanted the big one with him,
and so challenged Bo and John, the best I knew.
We tore through them the first set, 6-1,
but by the second on that stifling summer night
I was breathing cotton and every joint was on strike, yelling
"Your season's over!"

I fought, lumbered, felt his frustration and irritation,
my area of competence shrinking to one third of our space,
his growing in proportion.
Oddly, soaked with sweat,
I thought of us on ski slopes 13 years before.
Me, freezing, trying to reattach his bindings, torn
between wanting to sail down the delicious slopes alone,
and exulting in his growing competence.
I flashed back to endless "catches" and
fetching from the woods his wild pitches.

He managed somehow to bring us back to 5-5.
We lost 7-5.
But somewhere in there his face softened;
he began to encourage me.
Amid the frenzy of the battle
we were delivered to a quiet place
of understanding, of acceptance.

McLean, Virginia, September 1996

Miracle of
Grandchildren

Born Again

This tiny child,
   all of 7.4 pounds at birth,
   shouldering up the family's tectonic plates;
   realigning us,
   renaming us:
        my son now father
        my daughter now aunt
        my daughter-in-law now mother
        my wife and I now grandmother, grandfather.

This tiny child
   securing me a seat on the plane where there were no seats
   until I mentioned "…the birth of my first grandchild,"
   and first class at that with no additional charge.

This tiny child
   spurring the customer service agent in Dallas,
   a woman with beehived hair,
   to spread out pictures of her eight grandchildren
   smoothly as a Vegas dealer,
   and to tell me their names and birthdates
   while shifting me to an earlier "unavailable" connecting flight
   to my grandchild.

This tiny child,
   pulling smiles from total strangers,
   leading me to exult in thoughts of
   t-ball, piano, adventures in caves,
   expeditions to muddy construction sites,
   rough-housing, plays, reading, and more;
   galvanizing my wife to rearrange our house
   to welcome this new being.

This tiny child,
  curling her toes the size of infant peas;
  claiming no word, no sentience, no locomotion;
  fragile yet alive with flail.

This tiny child,
  unleashing love, the ultimate power,
  changing us forever;
  giving us all
  rebirth.

San Antonio, Texas, September 2006

Summer at the Beach

I get up early to get my e-mails
behind me,
because soon Lauren will bounce down stairs
before me.

And then
I will become the toast thief,
the monster who captures mermaids,
the seeker for the squealing hider,
the tornado maker who tosses rafts aloft,
the sandcastle assistant and seashell paver
the storyteller watched intently by wide eyes
poking just above the covers.

Shut the office door behind me!
Because now
       here
          only
             once
does one get to be the monster who catches mermaids.

Seize it!
Oh yes, seize it,
because all too soon
mermaids slip away.

Bethany Beach, Delaware, June 2010

Wondering Along

We

      go to the store
      see a monument
      visit a friend
      go to work
      get money from the ATM
      pick up some dinner.
Efficient and linear
we scurry unaware;
miracles under our noses,
miracles that Katie, two, and Lauren, four,
sniff out in an instant.

"What did you three guys do?" asks my daughter-in-law.
They crowd around her, shrieking the news:
"We walked on stone walls and Katie didn't fall,
even on the uneven stones…"
"I made Lalo laugh with tickle grass…"
"I made wet footprints from the sprinkler…"
"I made wet handprints but only three fingers came out…"
"I found a stone for you, mommy. It has red lines in it!"

I guess we made it about 150 yards up the street,
just wondering along.

Colorado Springs, Colorado, August 2010

To the Next Generation

The local weatherman called it a "wind burst,"
a term I hadn't heard.
Cyclone, hurricane, tornado, yes,
but not wind burst.
An explosion – fierce, focused air
slashing a tidy aisle 25 yards wide, 100 yards long;
tossing aside towering poplars as if twigs.

It happened in the vest-pocket park by our new house
the year we moved in,
the year I had my prostate operation.
The unruly stack of branches now dens a young fox family
who sit brazenly on the fallen timbers,
silent arrows aimed at unwary squirrels.

A tangle of thorn and briar,
led by young white pom-poms of the wild raspberry,
crowds the new corridor of light in the dense woods.

In spite of torn limbs
and a hole in the forest,
I revel in the flowers,
joyous sign of the next generation,
now parading in the gap.

Falls Church, Virginia, August 2008

Bethany Beach

Corn withering.
Geese flying south in amazing V formation –
an arrow pointed at my heart –
and in a smaller town near the beach resorts,
I notice only a white-haired man
guiding a bent woman in a walker slowly across the street.

I'm cheating.
Leaving my computer, meetings, site visits,
my wife dragging herself through one more year of teaching,
for one day, just one day in salt water riding waves.
Calvin, ever-present,
shakes his finger at me the whole drive down.

Few people.
The beaches eerily quiet, a bifurcated scattering
of gray hairs and young couples with infants in arms
(no volleyball, kites, bikinis, or Frisbees –
the hormone crowd is in school).
The water at its warmest, but no one swims,
choosing to sand at the edge,
staring out, writing thoughts on the vast ocean easel.

Tough summer.
Only four days' break: we helped both children move;
we ourselves are packing.
Writing, work, and houses claimed our days.
Two close friends lost – one to cancer, one to Alzheimer's.
Another now wears a colostomy bag.

Diving gulls
harass the lingering few.
Horse flies hover for a final meal.
The tide, low, flaccid, limps in.

A Lego-block freighter lumps along the horizon.
No low-flying planes drag noisy commercials.

It changes!
Suddenly the beach smattering stands,
pointing excitedly as dolphin fins cut the water
with miraculous ease,
an epiphany of grace and invisible power.

I dive in.
I think of the hours and days spent in the water
with my mother and father,
with my children (and yes, paddle ball and football and more,
always more…),
and now my grandchild;
my wife at shore's edge, carefully counting heads.

I swim.
And again swim, riding the waves in, then out,
now exulting, giving thanks for the salt tang of memories
and the incessant sea pushing me back to shore,
back to family and friends,
and to winter with salt in my mouth.

Bethany Beach, Delaware, September 2007

Sidewalk Cracks

She has her stroller full of animals.
I call them her zoo.
"It's not a zoo. They're my babies."

A sudden bump spills kitty to the concrete.
"Kitty's hurt," I say.
"Where?"
"On her left ear."
"Show me exactly."
She kisses kitty's left ear.
"Did you see any blood?"
"No, it was just a bump," she replies.

I tuck kitty under Mr. Elephant and Care Bear,
both perched on the stroller's plastic canopy.
"No, that's not where she goes."
"But she'll fall," I say. "I've made her safe."
"No. She can't see under Mr. Elephant.
She has to help me look for stones for mommy."

Colorado Springs landscapes with stones, you know.

"Lalo, can you hold my stroller? Kitty just saw a shiny stone."
She squats, pouring over marble sized pebbles.
She finds three. The mica gleams.
"Lalo, put them in your hand. Can you squeeze tight?"

We talk about her third birthday, which was yesterday.
She wants another, "Maybe tomorrow.
I want to be four tomorrow.
If I have green icing on my cake, will you come again?"

She squats at a small puddle made by a lawn sprinkler.
Her hand slaps the wet.
She rolls her stroller through it.
"Look, Lalo. My stroller makes lines."

We talk about chipmunks,
red birds, dinosaurs, party balloons, her purple tutu.
She climbs a neighbor's low stone wall,
walking the rim of the serpentine structure.
 "Lalo. Stand near me, but don't hold my hand."
She still wears her birthday crown
and a long necklace that almost trips her.
From the last stone she jumps,
her hands straight out from her sides.
She has watched the Olympics.

At the corner she stops and sort of looks.
"No cars, trucks, motorcycles or bicycles."
"Or elephants," I say.
"Or bears," she giggles.

Running now to get the shiny stone home to mom,
she hits the big crack.
All her animals now sprawl on the sidewalk.
"Wow, that was quite an accident, but I think they're all okay.
Let's put them back."
"No, Lalo. They're all hurt. Each one needs a kiss.
Mr. Elephant is really hurt.
Where does he hurt, Lalo, exactly?
I need to kiss the right place."
She heals all of them,
each with a careful kiss on the specified part:
toe, arm, ear, butt, foot, elbow, back.

I have a speech this week, two conference calls,
a proposal to write;
And a flight to catch, and a train to New York.
My world is context.

Not here. Stones, puddles, cracks.
Only discovery.

I see the chipped sidewalk anew --
a derailer of strollers,
a spiller of animals.
Although just 20 feet from the front door,
another planet.

Colorado Springs, Colorado, August 2009

The Armada Behind

At our 25th reunion, I wrote
        "We talk more of caulking than of conquest
        and we know that each has been there and is back.
        We have each faced typhoons; each known success,
        ecstasy,
        and the terror of sailing without compass."
Now we're back here at our 50th.
        The talk is of grandchildren:
        One flies across the country to see them.
        One has them every weekend.
        One coaches them.
        One cooks every weekday.
        One is raising them.
        Many move closer and
        all visit.
We're there again!
        Tiny, sticky hands in ours – again!
        A diaper to change – again!
        Gritty eyes as we read Doctor Seuss – again!
        The wonder of a leaf or rock – again!
        We rejoice in once-familiar context.
At sea,
        heaving to,
        climbing back into our boats
        (with pacemakers, bad backs, varicose veins, diabetes),
        steering gently,
        piloting only to warn of rough waters
        guiding to snug harbors.
We now,
        mother ships for all our grandchildren,
        the armada behind.

Falls Church, Virginia, October 2008

Portraits

George

It will be a swim of about
one mile,
from Alcatraz Island in 56-degree
water
to the shores of San Francisco, through vicious
cross-currents.

"I've been working toward something like this for
15 years.
Two, three times a week, 70-80 laps a day, more than
a mile."

The waves from the seismic shifts of
his past
had made swimming difficult. Sometimes even staying afloat
was hard.

The silt of his past could clog his eye,
crab his stroke,
past currents, rip tides,
yawing this intentional man off course.

Yet he never retreated to the safety
of the shore.
Rather, he went for the turbulence
where he kicked up the silt of his past.

He spurned the narcotic of Florida's
soporific seas,
wanting rather to confront the abuse
that had impeded him.

He swims now in wave and chop
aiming to disturb silt.
Kicking hard, swimming not above
but through.

He swims for himself,
for his past
and for those on shore,
still silt-clogged by their pasts.

Boston, Massachusetts, May 2008

Dirt

I am attracted to the people
that the poet Marge Piercy celebrates:
"I want to be with people who submerge in the task,
who go into the fields to harvest,
and work in a row and pass the bags along…
The pitcher cries for water to carry
and a person for work that is real."

But I would push further, beyond the useful end.
Through the work comes both product and meaning –
in the dirt,
not around it,
not over it,
not above it.

You cannot and should not transcend
the cares of the world.
It is only on the path, in the dirt, that one finds purpose.

Gospel singer Mahalia Jackson captures it:
"Keep your hand on the plow and your eyes on the stars."

You won't plow straight unless you have an eye on the stars.
Plowing means hands with splinters and blisters,
bloody hands given meaning
only because of the stars.

Salinas, California, September 2009

Rose

Rose begs on 17th Street.
She has her spot staked out,
just a few feet down from Starbucks,
sitting on her milk crate and cushion.
The homeless Vietnam vet and
the woman dying of AIDS do not encroach on her spot.

Rose has no teeth.
Her gums glisten in the morning sun.
Rose smells and wears a grab bag of clothes.
But Rose drinks Diet Coke:
"I must lose weight, you know."

The car carrying the son of a dear friend
driving down Route 95 to a soccer game,
was crushed by a dump truck that flipped,
killing the driver and his wife,
cracking the skull of my friend's son,
ripping synapses in a blink,
sending him from the eighth to first grade
and a slow (but successful) struggle back.

Rose, my talisman in whom I invest daily,
reminds me that
we hang by a thread,
none of us far
from a crate or a crash,
and to celebrate, celebrate,
as she drinks her Diet Coke,
a chalice to her femininity, not quite forgotten.

September, 1999, Washington, DC

A Sparrow at Dulles Airport

Barely contained chaos, anxiety
as the six snaked, chuted lines
inch toward the ticket counter.
The scrape of bags,
cacophony of cell phones,
crying children,
a collision of language, and, above the din
a shout, "Next, take 19. Next, take seven!" She,
pointing, directing.

Suddenly a sparrow
about the size of a crumpled Kleenex
lands in the small space between lines and counter,
wobbling.

The sparrow doesn't move.
Those near the sparrow stop.
The line stops.
Two ticket clerks and one bag handler
stop.

The sparrow has given up
banging against the seeming sky
of the immense glass roof.
Spent.

Our uniformed shunter,
pushing back a stray hank of brown hair
folding her list of departures into her back pocket,
gripping her pen in her teeth,
walking to the bird,
kneels.

Cupping her hands, as if under a faucet,
she lifts the bird—dazed, compliant—and
rises.

The crowd—wanting to cheer,
knowing it's not over,
holding its breath,
stepping aside for the shunter, now a priestess,
holding in her hand a shard of the divine—
parting the lines.

Now outside the door,
now beyond the sidewalk check-in;
now throwing her arms up and out,
as if giving dawn
welcome.

The bird is out! Up! Then maybe ten feet
then faltering, turning, spinning down
into the open trunk of a black limo.
Who, where, what!
The driver jumps back.

The priestess strides through his glare
to his trunk, cupping the bird again,
She walking, the crowd leaning, craning necks
Where is she taking it now? We can't see her!
She and the bird both
gone.

There is a sigh.
The shuffle and noise resume. The line
moves.
But for a moment, just for a moment
in the clang and push and strive
of our daily horizontal
comes a glimpse of the vertical
as an exhausted sparrow,
by alighting on our
closeted compassion,
stops us in our tracks.

Dulles International Airport, Virginia, September 2006

Musician on Boston's Blue Line

The guitarist sits on an upended milk crate.
His case, open at his feet, displays strewn coins
and three one dollar bills.
One is crumpled.
He doesn't see the money.
He doesn't see any of us in transit.
His eyes are closed.
He's playing Bach's Seventh Violin Concerto.
He's playing it with breathtaking virtuosity -
on the guitar! (Shhh).
Awed, riders have turned their backs on the tracks.

He's flawless until he picks one wrong note,
One amid the textured, fugal tangle.
One note.
Only one.
He winces, smiles, and whispers, "I'm sorry."
To whom, I wonder, is he apologizing?
To us? To Bach?
To an ideal that exists only in his head?
One missed note out of thousands.
Yet he has apologized, not out of deference to us, I think,
but to the sound that should be.

The train screeches in, as Boston's trains do.
A child, transfixed by the music, does not want to board.

How many strings do we pluck in life,
knowing our shortfall in the face of the ideal?

Our work is not to fall prostrate before the ideal,
collapsing in self-abnegation,
but rather to smile at the ideal saying, "Yes, yes, I know…"
and to keep on playing,
and playing.
Playing on.
And on.

Boston, Massachusetts, December, 2003

Of Curves

The grass was greener;
The uniforms blindingly white;
The smudges ground more deeply,
evoking battles harder fought.
The friendships and falling outs were eternal,
the breasts magnificent and stupefying,
and the curve of waist, flaring into hip, marked
the perimeter of endless speculation and chimerical bravado.
The occasional pedagogic seed that did take root
roared into blossoms of unassailable truth.

Three decades later we trace with fingers of memory
that gentle curve of life,
then electric with possibility,
now a break from flat trajectories.
Do we not work desperately to flatten the curves,
To hammer the lines into comfortable predictability—
> the perfect lawn,
> the right college,
> a bigger house,
> promotion?
Straight lines that can comfort,
that can imprison.

We are probably wise. Some have flown off the curve
into unbounded trajectories of terror:
separation, divorce, death of love and loved ones, loss of job.
Then why do we return?

College reunions are gatherings of boards of directors.
But to high school reune is to drink of that spring so long
unsipped,
of wonder, of discovery,

when all was tasted for the first time.
Why again?

Perhaps it is to recall the curve,
either as a memory,
a quiet liturgical blessing on what was,
or to embolden us to retrace our straight lines of now—
to probe for the hidden, magic curves
and (yes now here at almost 50)
to create new curves,
to rediscover wonder;
and to celebrate.
To celebrate.

Swarthmore, Pennsylvania, June 1988

Going and Coming

Going and Coming

Fat magnolia blossoms, gobs of vanilla ice cream
slashed by the sudden red of a cardinal.
"Can you say how long?"
The question neither good nor fair.
What difference does it make: an hour, a day, a week, a month?
Would I do anything differently? No.

She puts her medical bag into the back seat.
Six more hospice stops.
"We don't know. Mike's lost weight. But his spirit is good."
A wasp digs into the eaves of the garage.
"Why doesn't he eat?"
"His body doesn't have the energy to digest."
"I'll bring bar food next time. Potato skins"
"Wonderful, but only a few."

She wears a large cross. I wonder what it means to her.
"I believe in the resurrection of the body..."
His body now, the one with oxygen tubes?
Surely not. The body of four years ago,
clad in St. Patrick's Day green?
Or perhaps as a baby?

God is compassionate. He'd get to wear green.
"He has defeated sin and death..."
Too weak to sin.
We'll surround him with life.
God's got the next step.

"Name this child."
Granddaughter Katie's in her all-white Baptismal outfit.
Suddenly a hearty poop during the droning sermon.
A hasty exit; an equally quick return as the sermon ends.

"Do you put your whole trust in His grace and love?
Will you strive for justice and peace among all people,
and respect the dignity of every human being?
Teach them to love others in the power of the Spirit...
Send them into the world in witness to your love..."
We promise. The congregation promises.

Is it not ours to welcome both as new,
one tubed, one freshly diapered?
Lord, embrace her.
Lord, embrace him.
Lord, embrace us.
Lord, strengthen us
to embrace these lives
and daily to be amazed.

Colorado Springs, Colorado, April 2010

Incarnatus Est

He couldn't stop coughing.
After five minutes it stopped,
chin resting on his chest,
neck muscles too weak to support his head.

IN

"Anything we can do, Mike?"
"No. Rest. Breathe."
We had been getting together monthly
soon after his diagnosis 18 months before.
We usually met at McKeever's pub –
crowded, the way he liked it.
The waitress knew that one more undone button
would make old men smile.
We pretended to be hard of hearing.
She had to lean closer to take our order.
She knew.

INCAR

Then it was weekly at his house,
his strength waning, even with the oxygen tank.
"Mike, you only took one bite of your burger.
You left your French fries."
"I'm done.
Save it for Kim.
Brittany will love the fries.
Put them in the fridge."

INCARNATUS

Three years before, we, holding hands around her bed,

watched as cancer finished its work,
snatching the last breath
from his wife of forty years.
He remarried.
Kim entered his life with two teenagers.
The house was again as he loved it,
full of noise and streams of people.
"Guys, I can't drive Brit to school anymore.
No more coffee and hot chocolate for us at 7-11."
Soon thereafter came the diagnosis,
the reason for his mysterious shortness of breath.
IPF. Idiosyncratic pulmonary something.
"Incurable. You have two years give or take."
Then in January, three months ago,
"Four weeks to four months."

INCARNATUS ES

"Guys. Guys, I've got to go to bed.
I'm embarrassed. I know it's only 5:45. Earliest yet.
Stay. You know where the beer and vodka are."
We get him to bed.
"Good night, brother."
My hand on his shoulder.
I feel it would break if I squeezed hard.
"Good night, brother."

INCARNATUS EST

"And the Word was made flesh and dwelt among us."

What a precious gift, this flesh,
this flesh that makes no sense at all – none –
unless quickened by love and shared.
Is this not our job,
our only job, this sharing of such a gift?
That gift with which
            now,
                  at this time,
                        we are blessed.

Falls Church, Virginia, March 2010

Ledge

A curtain, descending over that lustrous mind,
that mind that drew rich laughter from almost everything;
that mind now expressed as pinched face, furrowed brow,
clenched jaw, all fighting to understand;
synaptic wires trying to find databases, swinging unplugged,
her face desperate to connect.
My son? Yes, my son. Lives? Lives? In New York!
He lives in New York!

They call it Alzheimer's. I call it theft.
Does the door we open shed light on darkening self
or throw too-harsh light on a befuddled present,
forcing her to wonder who she is now?

Cancer, too, she has,
the crab escaping her removed ovaries
to unknown parts of her body.
They will poison the waters in which the crab swims,
trying to stop its relentless scuttling.

Together we seek a safe resting spot,
a place clear of Alzheimer's and crabs,
if only a ledge, a solid place
(and if only for a little while),
a place where we can look at the beautiful, but dimming view,
or now close into each other's eyes:
better, yes, now into each other's eyes,
close enough to smooth that furrowed brow.

Is that not our task, to seek and to find,
however narrow,
that ledge?

Watertown, Massachusetts, March 2007

74

Scytheman

And so another friend calls,
this one in tears: "Jack, I have cancer."
Prominent, beloved, president of this and that,
a child advocate.
"But I've so much work to do. I'm not finished yet.
Not now."

And then an e-mail this morning: Erich has pancreatic cancer.
He has cancelled appearances in Detroit and Chicago.
He will not go to China.
He hopes to conduct the National Symphony twice -
on Memorial Day and the Fourth of July.

My prayer list grows. So many names.
I now have a list by my bed.
Deus ex machina is not my credo.
Rather I believe, "What can I do?"

Through which portal will the scytheman enter?
A cut as I chainsaw our winter wood supply?
My heart as I race from one meeting to the next?
My brain, a swift stroke disconnecting my wires?

Or bored with dramatic exits, he may simply dispatch
a microscopic emissary, who unannounced and undetected will
make traitors of my good blood cells.
(Such was the method he employed with my cousin,
his troops now feasting on her bone marrow.)

One thing is certain: he will win.
Or so he thinks.

What if I'm making love to my wife,
exulting with friends,
rolling on the floor with my grandkids,
having dinner with my daughter,
playing tennis with my son,
visiting a sick friend,
buried in Bach's Saint Matthew Passion,
working on a piece of legislation,
keynoting a youth conference,
planting my tomatoes,
writing this?

Then I would say this:
"Scytheman, I know you're there.
I know you'll reap me one day.
But it will take more than a tap on my shoulder,
because I'm not paying you any attention."
I won't be ready for you; I will be ripe,
busy loving.

McLean, Virginia, September 2008

76

Zyg

He's usually in a fetal position now.
His family has erected a small altar on the radiator:
A large picture of him and Marie, his wife of 68 years,
flanked by the altar vessels — Sprite, Gatorade, water.
By his bed medicines, the TV remote, another family picture.

When the Germans invaded, he fled Poland on foot,
often through knee-deep snows.
Somehow he found his wife,
she a refugee in Paris.

Then England,
then the U.S., the State Department;
occasional editorials for the New York Times,
and moderator for the Aspen Institute's Executive Seminars,
where we met, I his co-moderator;
he 80 percent and I 20 percent (his definition of "co").

This international man's world,
now shrunk to a 10 by 15 room
"Just hold his hand. Talk tires him," says daughter Maria.
I hold his liver-splotched hand,
his arm a chicken wing,
his pulse a flicker.

"You again. Why are you here?" he whispers.
"For the free lunch," I respond.
He smiles.
Our old banter.
Eyes open. Two sentences.
Eyes closed.
Then back to sleep.

He curls to a fetal position again:
Just a few wrinkles under the thin blanket.
I hold his hand, as one would a child's.
A child wails not for words,
but only to be held.

Has his cosmopolitan world shrunk?
No. We bask with him in the certainty and vastness of
steadfast love,
perhaps on the lip of the widest world
Zyg has ever known.

Washington, DC, September 12, 2010

Mother

The call came about midnight from Helen
who reported the massive stroke.
And we gathered the next day and saw her,
wires sundered.
The few remaining
kept the bare motor functions twitching.

And hundreds of others gathered, called, wrote.
(Even Harvey-from-England appeared at the hospital.)

People say how lucky we were to get there
in time to say goodbye.
But they were wrong, for we really gathered
to say hello.

Something we don't usually get right in life;
for saying goodbye
is not as risky as a full hello to the living.
Hello to life, the essence of her.

Haverford, Pennsylvania, April 1993

Imago Dei

She told me that she
fought through her fears
to go to the bedside of her estranged,
dying father.
"I cannot tell you how glad I was
to get to say goodbye."

She has it wrong, I thought:
Not "goodbye,"
but perhaps for the first time, "hello."

A friend who doctors prisoners
released to die of AIDS said,
"It's amazing. They change.
Their defenses drop.
Their personalities emerge like butterflies."

Should it really be easier to risk hello, risk our true selves,
when we know there's a quick exit,
the sure knowledge of death,
the ultimate hedge against rejection?
How odd that we feel protected by death, not life.

The armor of imminent death should not be needed;
rather we need the certain truth that we,
like the Velveteen Rabbit, should wind up
a bit battered,
wondrously worn,
sure in the knowledge that we're free to love,
because,
very simply,
we have been loved.

Boston, Massachusetts, August 1993

Acknowledgments

I t is a pleasure to record here my deep gratitude to those whose assistance has made this book possible.

The last several years I've been in the habit of writing a poem that accompanies our family's annual Christmas message. Several friends, most especially Pam Fiori, Editor of *Town & Country*, have said, "You must publish these poems." I thank Pam and the staff of *Town & Country* for publishing *Ledge,* one of my poems. On the other hand, when my kids were younger, the response I most often got was, "Dad, most normal people don't write poems on Christmas cards." As amazing adults, they now at least tolerate, if not forgive me this work, which in large part is a family chronicle.

Elinor Griffith, former Senior Editor at the *Reader's Digest,* brilliant editor of my first book, *Hope Matters: The Untold Story of How Faith Works in America,* and dear family friend, suggested, pushed, and, most often, encouraged.

When I served as President and CEO of the National Crime Prevention Council, Jean O'Neil worked for me for almost 20 years as Lead Editor and Researcher. With one of the most incisive pens and deepest understanding of almost anyone I know, Jean served as my prime editor. It's difficult to mess with poems, as the structures are fragile, structures that try to communicate a single thought, a single emotion. A comma here, a period there can and do make large differences. Jean's "tweaks" were laser-like.

I happened to meet Sue Gioulis by total accident. Staying at a small hotel (really a bed and breakfast) in Ocean Grove, N.J. close to the site of my wife's high school reunion, I had the pleasure of meeting Sue, who was working part time on the desk. She radiated warmth and interest. We spoke a bit, then at length. Turns out she was a local artist; but not so local, as she had illustrated a few children's books. I sent her a few drafts, and she sent me a few drawings. Amazingly fortuitous that we met: her drawings nailed the spirit, the grace, the tenderness.

Jeremy Kay, Publisher at Bartleby Press, assisted with editing, and with his fine eye, designed how this book would look. To Greg Giroux, editorial assistant at Bartleby Press, for his endless patience in formatting, reformatting, and assistance with editing, I give my heartfelt thanks.

The most special tributes I reserve for my family: my children, Hollis and Byron Calhoun, his wife Allyssa and their kids, my grandkids, Lauren and Katie. Ottilia, my wife of 39 years deserves special recognition for enduring the long nights, early mornings, and weekends I spent writing, taking time from us and other pursuits, and having faith that this book would see the light of day and would move others. Each in their own way served as muses for most of these poems, muses that inspired me, and I hope, you.